WHAT IF I FEEL FAINT?

JAN 2 – 2017

Gareth Stevens
PUBLISHING

BY AMY HAYES

Please visit our website, www.garethstevens.com. For a free color catalog of all our high-quality books, call toll free 1-800-542-2595 or fax 1-877-542-2596.

Cataloging-in-Publication Data

Names: Hayes, Amy.
Title: What if I feel faint? / Amy Hayes.
Description: New York : Gareth Stevens Publishing, 2017. | Series: Benched: dealing with sports injuries | Includes index.
Identifiers: ISBN 9781482448931 (pbk.) | ISBN 9781482448870 (library bound) | ISBN 9781482448405 (6 pack)
Subjects: LCSH: Sports injuries–Juvenile literature. | Sports injuries in children–Juvenile literature. | Syncope (Pathology)
Classification: LCC RD97.H39 2017 | DDC 617.1'027–dc23

First Edition

Published in 2017 by
Gareth Stevens Publishing
111 East 14th Street, Suite 349
New York, NY 10003

Copyright © 2017 Gareth Stevens Publishing

Designer: Katelyn E. Reynolds
Editor: Ryan Nagelhout

Photo credits: Cover, p. 1 (background photo) J. Helgason/Shutterstock.com; cover, p. 1 (girl) CebotariN/Shutterstock.com; cover, pp. 1–24 (background texture) mexrix/Shutterstock.com; cover, pp. 1–24 (chalk elements) Aleks Melnik/Shutterstock.com; p. 5 TinnaPong/Shutterstock.com; p. 7 Alila Medical Media/Shutterstock.com; p. 9 Oleg Mikhaylov/Shutterstock.com; pp. 11, 19 Pavel L Photo and Video/Shutterstock.com; p. 13 (girl) princessdlaf/E+/Getty Images; p. 13 (background) sharpshutter/Shutterstock.com; p. 15 Fuse/Getty Images; p. 17 Emil Pozar/age fotostock/Getty Images; p. 21 Jamie Squire/Getty Images.

Printed in the United States of America

CPSIA compliance information: Batch #CS16GS : For further information contact Gareth Stevens, New York, New York at 1-800-542-2595.

CONTENTS

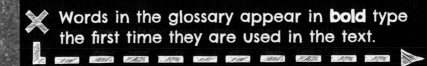

Words in the glossary appear in bold type the first time they are used in the text.

A BIT LIGHT-HEADED

It's a hot day, and the sun is shining. You're running really fast toward the finish line. Suddenly, you don't feel well. Your head feels like it's swimming through water. Your hearing begins to shut down, and you're very **dizzy**. You even feel a rush of heat.

What's going on? You're feeling faint! Fainting and dizziness are very common in sports, especially in teenagers and children. While fainting can be **serious**, it doesn't always mean there's a problem.

FEELING FAINT?

Here are some things that might happen before you faint:

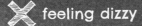 feeling dizzy

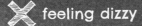 seeing spots

 hearing ringing sounds

 feeling sick to your stomach

 feeling hot or cold

 increased heart rate

 becoming pale

If you aren't feeling right, stop playing and talk to someone right away.

✗ THE GAME PLAN

If a person faints, they should only be **unconscious** for 1 or 2 minutes. If the fainting spell lasts longer, call a doctor right away.

5

NOT ENOUGH BLOOD

Fainting and dizziness are both caused by the brain not getting things it needs to work properly. Our brain needs **oxygen** to work. Blood carries oxygen to our brain. When the brain doesn't get enough blood, it doesn't have enough oxygen to operate. We begin to feel dizzy.

Sometimes, if the brain really doesn't have enough blood, we begin to feel weak and even lose consciousness. When a person loses consciousness, we say they've fainted.

Even though the brain is just 2 percent of a person's body weight, it needs 15 to 20 percent of the body's blood supply.

internal
carotid
arteries

vertebral
arteries

Blood enters the brain through two pairs of **blood vessels**. They're called the internal carotid arteries and the vertebral arteries.

FOOD AND WATER

Some of the main reasons people feel faint are not eating enough or drinking enough. When a person doesn't eat enough food or drink enough water, they're more likely to faint.

When a person doesn't drink enough water, they can become **dehydrated**. Dehydration is common when it's very hot outside and you lose a lot of **fluids** by sweating. Dehydration can lower **blood pressure**, which leads to feeling faint. To prevent this, drink lots of water on hot days and before and during exercise.

Staying hydrated will make you a stronger, more aware athlete!

9

JUST GROWING

Young bodies grow pretty fast—they get taller and often need new clothes. When a body experiences **puberty**, it kicks into high gear and grows very fast. When the body is so focused on changing and growing, it can sometimes act a little strange.

Blood pressure in young people during puberty can get very low. This is one reason why it's pretty common for tweens and teens to feel dizzy or faint.

✗ THE GAME PLAN

Since growing young people go through so many changes, you might not even know you haven't been drinking enough water or eating enough food. ▶

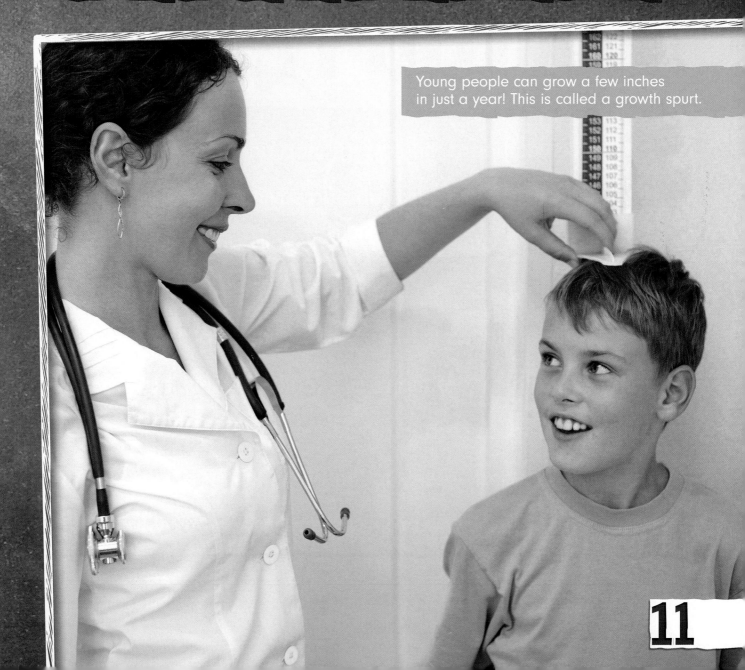

Young people can grow a few inches in just a year! This is called a growth spurt.

11

BREATHING TOO FAST

Have you heard the saying "stop and catch your breath"? It might seem like an odd saying, but it's important to breathe properly, especially during hard exercise. Otherwise, you might hyperventilate.

Hyperventilating is when you breathe too quickly and breathe out more than you breathe in. This leaves you with too much carbon dioxide in your blood. That narrows the blood vessels to the brain, thus reducing the amount of blood to the brain. As a result, you may faint.

✖ THE GAME PLAN

1 If you start to hyperventilate, try breathing in and out through your nose. If that doesn't work, focus on holding your breath for a few seconds. Both will slow down your breathing.

People hyperventilate for many reasons—losing breathing **rhythm** while working out, **stress**, fear, or a huge shock can all cause a person to start breathing too fast.

LET
SOMEONE KNOW

So now you know why people feel faint. But what do you do if you start to feel dizzy and think a fainting spell might be coming during a game?

The first thing you should do is stop playing. Get to the bench or sideline and tell a coach or other adult what is going on. Tell them how you're feeling and any **symptoms** you might have. Don't go back into the game unless the feeling goes away.

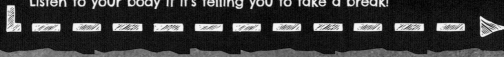

✕ THE GAME PLAN

Feeling faint or dizzy can often happen if you play hard during games, but sometimes it's a sign of something more serious. Listen to your body if it's telling you to take a break!

It's okay to take yourself out of a game if you don't feel good or get hurt. Your coach and teammates want healthy players out there!

STAYING CONSCIOUS

Fainting can feel pretty scary, but try to keep calm. There are several things you can do to help yourself. First of all, sit down. This will keep you from hurting yourself by falling if you actually faint. Next, put your head down between your knees. This will help blood reach your brain.

Another choice is to lie down. Don't get up until you start to feel better. If you're wearing tight clothing, try to loosen it.

1. If a person is nearby, ask them to bring you some water or a sports drink, which has salt in it. Make sure to sip it slowly. You might also want to eat something.

"Syncope" (SIHNG-kuh-pee) is the word doctors use to describe fainting.

TIME FOR THE DOCTOR

Most of the time, fainting isn't a sign of something seriously wrong. It can be something as simple as standing up too fast. Feeling faint could even mean you just need a drink.

Fainting regularly, however, can be a sign of trouble. If this happens, make sure you go to a doctor right away. They need to do tests to see what the problem is. Fainting can be linked to problems with other body parts such as the heart.

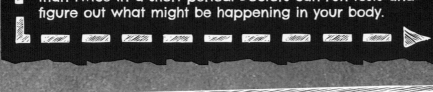

1. Make sure you go to a doctor if you've fainted more than twice in a short period. Doctors can run tests and figure out what might be happening in your body.

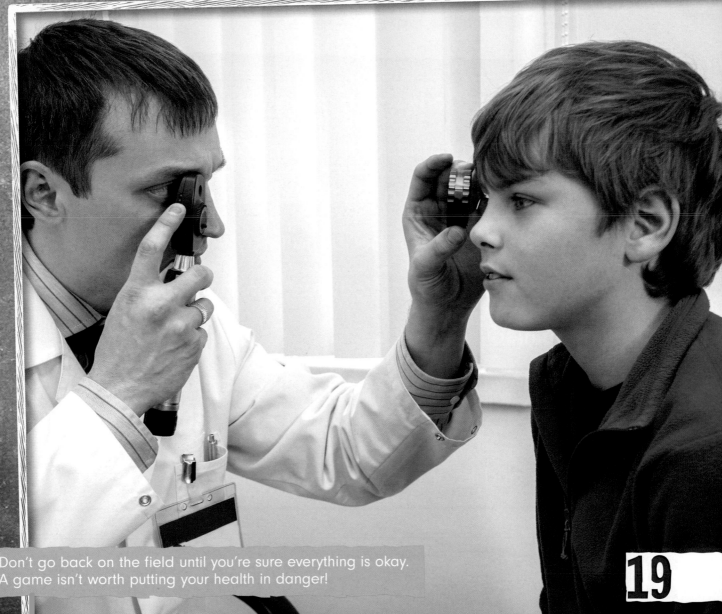

Don't go back on the field until you're sure everything is okay. A game isn't worth putting your health in danger!

19

CODY GOES DOWN

In 2004, Dan Cody was a defensive end for the University of Oklahoma football team. While on the sidelines, he was giving a big talk to his teammates. But as he was talking, he began to sway. As the team headed back to the field, Cody lost consciousness. He had fainted!

Cody's fainting spell was caught on camera. Two of his teammates helped him up. He was given some fluids and later returned to the game.

✗ THE GAME PLAN

After college, Cody went on to play in the National Football League for the Baltimore Ravens.

Some people worried Cody returned to the field before doctors could check on him. He had some fluids and didn't faint again, but it could have been something more serious.

GLOSSARY

blood pressure: the pressure of the blood on the walls of the blood vessels

blood vessel: a small tube that carries blood through the body

dehydrated: the condition of not having enough fluids in the body

dizzy: having a feeling of spinning

fluid: a liquid

oxygen: a colorless gas humans need to breathe to live

puberty: a time of change when children grow into adults

rhythm: an ordered pattern that repeats

serious: something important

stress: worry or fear of something

symptom: a change in the body that shows something is wrong

unconscious: not awake or aware, especially because of injury

FOR MORE INFORMATION

BOOKS

Basen, Ryan. *Injuries in Sports*. Minneapolis, MN: ABDO Publishing, 2014.

Martin, Bobi. *The Muscles in Your Body*. New York, NY: Britannica Educational Publishing, 2015.

WEBSITES

Fainting
commonsportsinjuries.com/fainting
Learn more about fainting here.

I Got Dizzy Playing Sports: What's Going On?
kidshealth.org/en/teens/sports-dizzy.html
Find out more about why you might feel faint when you play sports here.

INDEX